Stem Cell Treatment for you-2015

A Reference for Physicians, Patients and a review of International Stem Cell Treatment Centers

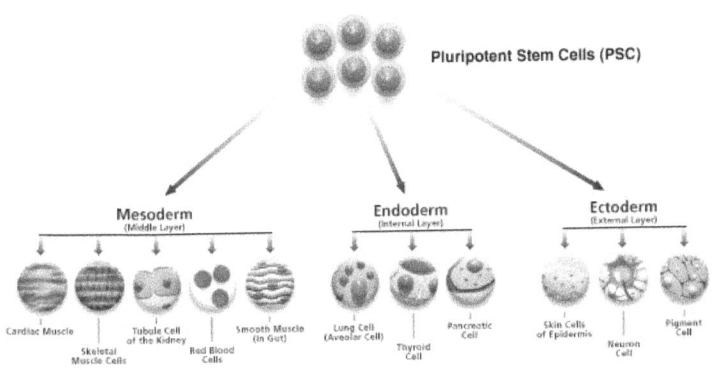

Pluripotent Stem Cells (PSC)

Mesoderm (Middle Layer)

Endoderm (Internal Layer)

Ectoderm (External Layer)

Cardiac Muscle

Skeletal Muscle Cells

Tubule Cell of the Kidney

Red Blood Cells

Smooth Muscle (In Gut)

Lung Cell (Aveolar Cell)

Thyroid Cell

Pancreatic Cell

Skin Cells of Epidermis

Neuron Cell

Pigment Cell

Dan M. Gama

Table of Contents

Chapter 1

Introduction

A stem cell is a kind of undifferentiated cell that has a unique capacity to renew itself and to give rise to specialized cell types of a different tissue. Although most cells of the body such as heart cells or skin cells are committed to conduct a specific function, a stem cell is uncommitted and remains uncommitted, until it receives a signal to develop into a specialized cell. Researchers have for years looked for ways to use stem cells for therapeutic possibilities to replace cells and tissues that are damaged or diseased. This research has yielded a glimpse at a class of stem cells that can develop into any cell type in the body. This class of stem cells is called pluripotent, meaning the cells have the potential to renew themselves, differentiate and develop to almost all of the more than 200 different known cell types, stem cells with this unique property come from embryos and fetal tissue.

In 1998, investigators were able to isolate this class of pluripotent stem cell from early human embryos and grew them in culture, they may have the potential to generate replacement cells for a broad array of tissues and organs such as the heart, pancreas and the nervous system. This class of human stem cells hold the promise in regenerative medicine of being able to repair or replace cells or tissues that are damaged or destroyed by many of devastating diseases and disability.

A stem cell from the embryo, fetus or adult that has under certain conditions has the ability to reproduce itself for longer periods or in the case of adult stem cells, throughout the life of the organism.

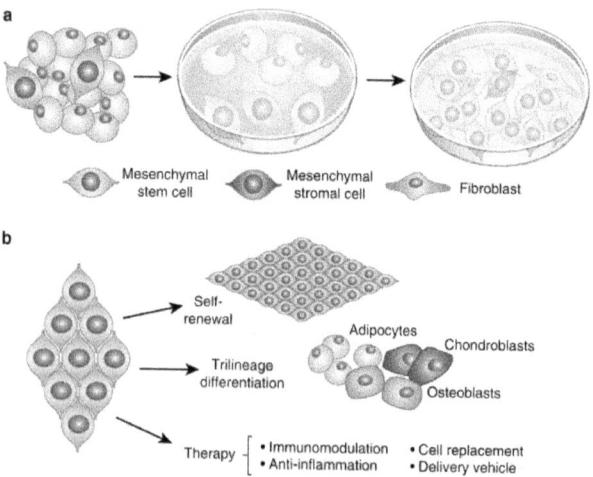

Figure 1. An example of Adipose Tissue Stem Cells in culture for therapeutic use

Embryonic Stem Cells

An embryonic stem cell is derived from a group of cells called the inner cell mass, which is part of the early (4 to 5 days) embryo development called the blastocyst stage. Once removed from the blastocyst, the cells of the inner cell mass can be cultured to produce embryonic cells. These embryonic stem cells are not themselves embryos. Evidence is emerging that these cells do not behave in the laboratory as they would in the developing embryo.

Adult Stem Cells

An adult stem cell is thought to be an undifferentiated (unspecialized) cell that occurs in a differentiated (specialized) tissue or organ that can renew itself, and become specialized to yield all of the specialized cell types of the tissue or organ from which it originated. Adult stem cells are capable of making identical copies of themselves for the lifetime of the organism. This property is referred to as ''self renewal'' Adult stem cells usually divide to generate progenitor or precursor cells, which then differentiate or develop into mature cell types that have characteristic shapes and specialized functions, e.g., muscle contraction or nerve cell signaling. Sources of adult stem cells include bone marrow, blood, the cornea and the retina of the eye, brain, skeletal muscle, dental pulp, liver, skin, the lining of the gastrointerstinal tract, and pancreas.

The most abundant information about adult human stem cells come from studies of hematopoietic stem cells isolated from the bone marrow and blood. These adult stem cells have been extensively studied and applied therapeutically for various diseases.

Stem Cell Transplantation Research

Stem cells may hold the key to replacing cells lost in many devastating diseases. Some diseases included in stem cell research include Parkinson's disease, diabetes, chronic heart disease, end-stage kidney disease, liver failure, and cancer, these are just a few for which stem cells have therapeutic potential. The goal is to find a way to replace what natural processes have taken way. Science has brought us to a point where the immune response can be subdued, so that organs from one person can be used to replace the diseased organs and tissues of another. But, despite recent advances in transplantation sciences, there is a shortage of donor organs that makes it unlikely that the growing demand for lifesaving organ replacements will be fully met through organ donation strategies.

The use of stem cells to generate replacement tissues for treating neurological diseases is a major focus of research. Spinal cord injury, multiple sclerosis, Parkinson's disease, and Alzheimer's disease are among those diseases for which the concept of replacing destroyed and dysfunctional cells in the brain or spinal cord is a practical goal.

Another major discovery frontier for research on adult and embryonic stem cells is the development of transplantable pancreatic tissue that can be used to treat diabetes. Researchers have recently shown that human embryonic stem cells to be directly differentiated into cells that produce insulin. The lines of unaltered human embryonic stem cells that exist will not be suitable for direct use in patients. These cells will need to be differentiated or otherwise modified before they can be used clinically. Current challenges are to direct the differentiation of embryonic stem cells into specialized cell populations and also to devise ways to control their development or proliferation once placed in patients.

Embryonic stem cells will undoubtedly be key as research tools for understanding fundamental events in embryonic development that one day may explain the causes of birth defects and approaches to correct or prevent them. Another important area of research that links developmental biology and stem cell biology is understanding genes and molecules, such as growth factors and nutrients, that function during the development of the embryo so that they can be used for growing stem cells in the laboratory and direct their development into specialized cell types.

Stem Cells as Therapeutic Delivery System

Stem cells are already being explored as a vehicle for delivering genes to specific tissues in the body. Stem cells based therapies are a major area of investigation in cancer research. For many years, restoration of blood and immune system function has been used as a component in the care of cancer patients who have been treated with chemotherapeutic agents. Now researchers are trying to devise more ways to use specialized cells derived from stem cells to target specific cancerous cells and directly deliver treatments that will destroy or modify them as seen in figure 2 below.

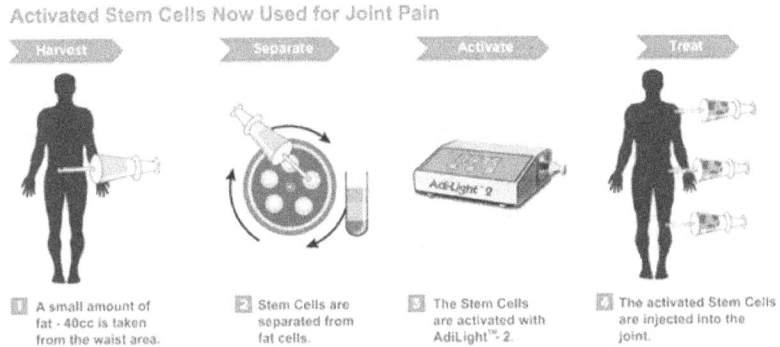

Figure 2. A schematic diagram of one type of stem cell therapy procedure.

The Purpose for this book

The new discovery of healing systems within the body opens up a whole new vision for treating diseases. We all have a banking facility for autologous stem cells within our bodies, in our bone marrow, fat and other areas. These cells are called upon to heal injuries or debilitating diseases. As we age, the reserves of stem cells within our bone marrow and fat begin to diminish. When we do not have enough stem cells to address illnesses or injury, symptoms occur, and we no longer effectively heal with chronic illness being the result. The process of extracting stem cells from the bone marrow or fat and re-introducing them in adequate numbers into the body allows the body to heal as it is meant to, naturally.

Most countries of the world look up to the United States of America (USA) as a pace setter for all things, could it be democracy, human rights, technology, health ethics etc. This directly means that if for some reason, the USA does not allow certain procedures to be practiced in the US, most countries will not feel comfortable practicing those in their own countries. This is exactly what has happened with the use of stem cells in therapy, regardless of so many research studies showing that the use of stem cells in therapy is safe and effective (adult stem cells), the Food and Drug Administration (FDA) has from time and time again denied Scientist and Doctors in America to legally use adult stem cells as means for curing a wide variety of diseases.

Scientists and Doctor's concerns are that the stem cells they are being denied to use are autologous stem cells, these are cells extracted from the patient who seek treatment, these cells are expanded to reach therapeutic dose and re-infused to the same patient they were extracted from. The FDA's responsibility is to regulate the proper use of drugs, of recent, the FDA has said that autologous stem cells should be regulated as drugs. This has coursed confusion for Scientists, Doctors and patients alike as to how can cells taken from an individual pose a medical concern when those cells are re-infused to the same individual.

The FDA's decision to regulate autologous stem cells has led to most Doctors moving their stem cell treatment centers to set up shop outside the USA. There are now hundreds of stem cell treatment centers (clinics) around the world providing treatment to a variety of diseases in countries where the regulatory laws against the use of autologous stem cells are not as strict as in the USA.

The purpose of this book is to provide information or reference to both patients and Doctors about stem cells, and stem cell treatment centers around the world, such information includes countries where the centers are located, physical addresses, contact persons, treatment cost, sources of stem cells used in treatment, type of diseases/conditions being treated and the protocols or procedures used. This reference will work as a quick guide to recommended stem cell treatment centers that can address their relevant needs. Doctors will be able to refer their patients to a relevant treatment center and patients will know about the protocols used, source of stem cells and the treatment cost so that they can properly plan for their treatment.

Chapter 2

Stem Cell Expansion

Adult stem cell (ASC) therapy represent a promising treatment modality in regenerative medicine and tissue engineering. The challenge with ASC use in therapy is the fact that they are found in very small numbers. For them to reach therapeutic dose, the number of stem cells should not be less than 2×10^6 stem cells. In order to overcome this limitation, there is need to expand the number of ASC to manufacturing scale to benefit people and patients with different medical conditions.

One way to achieve this is through culture methods, this has faced challenges because the culture media used has little potential of supporting their growth, hence the need to add growth factors, some of which include animal extracts like fetal bovine serum (FBS). The disadvantages with xenogenic serum is complicated because of high lot-to-lot variability and is associated with a risk of transmitting infectious agents and immunizing effects. In some cases, immunological reactions and anti-FBS antibodies have been observed and considered as having possibly affected the therapeutic outcome.

In order to overcome these challenges, there are promising studies that have demonstrated that for clinical scale manufacturing of ASCs, human factors from serum or platelets have been suggested as alternatives to FBS. In other studies, pooled human serum (HS) and thrombin-activated platelet releasate in plasma (tPRP) support the expansion of adipose tissue-derived Mesenchymal (MSCs) cells. In a study conducted by *Karen Bieback et al* 2009, their results showed that MSC population doublings and expansion kinetics were significantly enhanced in pHPL-supplemented BM-MSC culture compared with cultures supplemented with selected FBS.

Platelet-rich plasma (PRP) has gained importance in bone regeneration and healing since the α-granules of the platelets are rich in growth factors such as the vascular endothelial growth factors (VEGF), platelet-derived growth factor (PDGF) and transforming growth factor β (TGF-β) which play a key role in tissue healing.

In another study conducted by *Melanie Vogl et al* 2013, where the purpose of the study was to investigate whether tPR is able to increase the proliferation of MSCs especially MSCs of elderly donors. The supernatant of thrombin-activated platelet-rich plasma, the platelet releasate was found to be an excellent adjuvant in isolating and expanding human MSCs. The study also showed that tPR from pooled PRP influences significantly the proliferation of the MSC of young and mid-aged patients. The best proliferation rates were reached by adding 5% tPR. MSCs from old patients, there was a trend in proliferation increase after the addition of Trp.

One of the breakthroughs in the use of autologous stem cell in therapy is the ability to expand them using autologous serum. A number of research studies including the one conducted by *Akimoto Nimura et* al 2010, which examined whether heat-inactivation of serum affected the proliferation and whether autologous human serum influenced their multipotentiality made the use of human serum recommended for clinical use. Akimoto indicated that increasing the safety of medical treatments with MSCs requires the use of autologous human serum, in his study, he discovered that autologous human serum significantly increased the proliferation of synovial MSCs in contrast, compared with fetal bovine serum.

Autologous serum/plasma has successfully been used as a stem cell expansion supplement for in vitro culture of CD34+ cord blood, and proliferation of hematopoietic progenitor cells was markedly increased with serum supplements taken 4 or 8 days before HSCs implantation. To prove the significance of autologous/pooled human plasma, analysis of platelet releasates, lysates and sub-cellular fractions has shown that numerous bioactive molecules are stored within distinct platelet organelles including adhesive proteins, coagulation factors, mitogens, protease inhibitors and proteoglycans. Compared with serum, Buffy coat-derived platelet preparations are of particular interest because they do not complete with Red Blood Cells and plasma preparation for the limited available blood donations.

Automated Stem Cell Expansion

The large number of ex vivo expanded cells that are required in many clinical cell protocols greater than two million cells ($2x10^6$) per patient makes standard culture conditions problematic and expensive, resulting in need for extensive personnel and facilities resources and the potential for contamination. To meet such clinical demand, a robust automated and closed cell expansion method is optimal .

Specific steps taken to multiply the number of stem cells for re-implantation include; isolation of the stem cells from the patient's blood sample, by manual procedures or automated, e.g.; by using the Res-Q 60 BMC System (from CESCA Therapeutics). After isolation, the stem cells are counted (using hemocytometer etc) to determine cell density and viability, the cells can now be expanded by use of specific culture media (StemPro-34, StemSpan H2000 for HSCs). At this stage, the patient's scrum/plasma can be incorporated into the expansion culture media as supplement to provide required nutrients. The cultures are incubated at 37°C for 7-14 days. After incubation, the cultures are removed and the cells are counted and prepared for implantation. An expected number of HSC at the end of the expansion process is two million cells a number required to achieve a therapeutic dose .

Chapter 3

Sources of Stem Cells

For many years, researchers have been seeking to understand the body's ability to repair and replace the cells and tissues of some organs, but not others. After years of work pursuing the how and why of seemingly indiscriminant cell repair mechanisms, scientists have now focused their attention on adult stem cells. It has long been known that stem cells capable of renewing themselves and that they can generate multiple cell types.

Today, there is new evidence that stem cells are present in far more tissues and organs than once thought and that these cells are capable of developing into more kinds of cells than previously imagined. Efforts are now underway to harness stem cells and to take advantage of this new found capability, with the goal of devising new and more effective treatments for a host of diseases and disabilities. What lies ahead for the use of adult stem cells is unknown, but it is certain that there are many research questions to be answered and that these answers hold great promise for the future.

Like all stem cells, adult stem cells share two characteristics, they can make identical copies of themselves for long period of time, this ability is called long-term self-renewal. Adult stem cells can also give rise to mature cell types that have characteristic morphologies and specialized functions. ASCs are dispersed in tissues throughout the mature animal and behave very differently, depending on their local environment, for example, hematopoietic stem cells (HSCs) are constantly being generated in the bone marrow where they differentiate into mature types of blood cells.

Unlike embryonic stem cells which are defined by their origin (inner cell mass of the blastocyst), ASCs share no such definitive means of characterization. No one knows the origin of ASCs in any mature tissue. Definitions of ASCs vary in the scientific literature range from a single description of the cells to a rigorous set of experimental criteria that must be met before characterizing particular cell as an adult stem cell. The list of adult tissues reported to contain stem cells includes bone marrow, peripheral blood, brain, spinal cord, dental pulp, blood vessels, skeletal muscle, epithelia of the skin and digestive system, cornea, retina and pancreas.

ASCs should be clonogenic, a single ASC should be able to generate a line of genetically identical cells, which then give rise to all the appropriate differentiated cell types of which it resides. An ASC should also be able to give rise to fully differentiated cells that have mature phenotypes, are fully integrated into the tissue. Phenotype refers to all the observable characteristics of a cell, interactions with other cells and the non-cellular environment, proteins that appear on the cell surface and the cell behavior.

In order to fully characterize the regenerating and self-renewal capabilities of the ASC, and therefore truly harness its potential, it will be important to demonstrate that a single ASC can generate a line of genetically identical cell types of the tissue in which it resides.

If ASCs are to be prepared for therapeutic application, there should be evidence that there are ASCs present in the cell preparation. There are three methods used to determine whether candidate ASCs give rise to specialized cells. ASCs can be labeled in vivo and then they can be tracked. Candidate ASCs can also be isolated and labeled and then transplanted back into the organism to determine what becomes of them. Finally, candidate adult stem cells can be isolated, grown in vitro and manipulated, by adding growth factors or introducing genes that help determine what differentiated cells types they will yield. For an example, currently, Scientists believe that stem cells in the fetal and adult brain divide and give rise to nerve cells, of which there are many types.

It is often difficult to distinguish adult tissue-specific stem cells from progenitor cells, which are found in fetal or adult tissues and are partly differentiated cells that divide and give rise to differentiated cells. These are cells found in many organs that are generally thought to be present to replace cells and maintain the integrity of the tissue.

To be able to claim that ASCs demonstrate plasticity, it is first important to show that a cell population exists in the starting tissue that has the identifying features of stem cells. Then it is necessary to show that the ASCs give rise to cell types that normally occur in a different tissue. Proving the existence of an ASC population in a differentiated tissue is a laborious process. It requires that the candidate stem cells are shown to be self-renewing, and that they can give rise to the differentiated cell types that are characteristic of the tissue.

To show that ASCs can generate other cell types requires them to be tracked in their new environment, whether be it in vitro or in vivo. In general, this has been accomplished by obtaining the stem cells from a mouse that has been genetically engineered to express a molecular tag in all its cells. It is then necessary to show that the labeled ASCs have adopted key structural and biochemical characteristics of the new tissue they claim to have generated. It is necessary to demonstrate that the cells can integrate into their new tissue environment, survive in the tissue and function like the mature cells of the tissue.

Cord Blood

Cord blood is a sample of blood taken from a newborn baby's umbilical cord. It contains a rich source of stem cells, which could potentially be used in the treatment over 75 different diseases, including leukemia, lymphoma and anemia. Many expecting parents choose to bank their newborn's cord blood, as it may be useful in the future, should the child or a related family member fall victim to a disease that is potentially treatable by cord blood stem cells. Cord blood is obtained by syringing out the placenta through the umbilical cord at the time of childbirth, after the cord has been detached from the newborn. Cord blood is collected because it contains stem cells including hematopoietic cells, which can be used to treat hematopoietic and genetic disorders. One unit of cord blood generally lacks stem cells in a quantity sufficient to treat an adult patient.

The original clinically attractive feature of cord blood was the high concentration of hematopoietic stem cells, which is similar to that found in bone marrow 0.1-0.8 CD34+ cells per 100 nucleated cells. In addition to being a source of hematopoietic cells, cord blood contains potent angiogenesis stimulating cells. The CD34+, CD11b+ fraction, which is approximately less than half of the CD34+ fraction of cord blood which was demonstrated to possess ability to differentiate into functional endothelial cells in vitro and in vivo.

In addition to endothelial progenitors, mesenchymal stem cells found in cord blood are known to secrete numerous cytokines and growth factors such as VEGF and FGF-2 which stimulate angiogenic processes. Mesenchymal stem cells are capable of differentiating into various non-hematopoietic tissues. Mesenchymal stem cells are classically defined as capable of adhering to plastic and expressing a non-hematopoietic cell surface phenotype consiting of CD34-, CD45-, HLA-DR-, while possessing markers such as STRO-1, VCAM, CD13, CD29, CD44, CD90, CD105, SH-3. Mesenchymal stem cells have been purified from bone marrow, adipose tissue, placenta, scalp tissue and cord blood-derived mesenchymal stem cells have demonstrated the ability to differentiate into a wide variety of tissues in vitro including neuronal, hepatic, osteoblastic and cardiac.

An important aspect of this cell population is their anti-inflammatory and immunomodulator activity. For example, they constitutively secrete immune inhibitory cytokines such as IL-10 and TGF-β while maintaining ability to present antigens to T cells, thus suggesting they may act as a tolerogenic antigen presenting cell. Cells with markers and activities resembling embryonic stem cells have been found in cord blood. A population of CD34- cells expressing OCT-4, Nanog, SSEA-3 and SSEA-4, which could differentiate into cells of the mesoderm, ectoderm and endoderm lineage have been identified.

In the 1930s, it was reported that cord blood could be safely used as a substitute for peripheral blood for performing transfusions. Since HLA-matching was not available at that time and no adverse effects were noted. A resent lancet publication described the use of cord blood as a source of blood donation for malaria infested regions in Africa where 85 ml of ABO matched cord blood with no HLA matching. No report of graft versus host was noted.

Bone marrow and Peripheral Blood

The constant and continued supply of blood and its components to body tissues and organs is dependent on the constant and continued production and replenishing of the same. We know that all blood cells have a life span, for example, red blood, have a life span of 120 days, after which they are destroyed as they pass through the spleen. This means that these cells should be replaced by new ones. The system that does that is called the Hematopoietic System.
An average human requires approximately one hundred billion new hematopoietic cells each day. The continued production of these cells depends directly on the presence of the Hematopoietic Stem Cells (HSCs), ultimate and the only source of these cells. For decades, treatment for hematopoietic disorders has been by bone marrow transplant, however, this has encountered various limitations including the issue of Graft versus Host disease and the transmission of viruses like Cytomegalo Virus (CMV) and in-availability of donors etc.

Apart from being used to correct hematopoietic disorders, bone marrow is also used for cartilage repair because of its abundance in stromal cells also known as Mesenchymal stem cells which play a major role in cartilage repair, amongst its many functions. Since the procedure for obtaining a bone marrow sample is labor intensive as it requires recipient and donor tissue matching, and it is a very invasive procedure because the donor is put under anesthesia and a big needle is drilled to the hipbone or sternum to get a sample. Scientists have looked into possibilities of avoiding the painful procedure by demonstrating the presence of MSCs in peripheral blood, which can then be used as the procedure for harvesting whole blood (peripheral) is easy, less painful and quick compared to bone marrow harvesting procedures. bone marrow being the only tissue containing MSCs. *Roufosse et al* mentions that during tissue damage, MSCs are transported from the bone marrow to the damaged site via circulating peripheral blood to promote regeneration . This means that it is possible to get MSCs in peripheral blood. Using the procedure known as Blood mobilization using Granulocyte colony stimulating factor (G-CSF) increases the number of MSCs in peripheral blood. It has also been demonstrated that this technique does not selectively produce MSCs but rather a mix of MSCs. Bone marrow stromal cells generate cartilage, bone, and fat. *Yuji Takahara et al* carried experiments that proved the restorative effects of Adipose-derived mesenchymal Stem Cells on damaged ovarian function, this proves that MSCs can also be derived from Adipose tissue, not only in the bone marrow.

CD34 is a cluster of differentiation molecule present on certain cells within the human body. It is a cell surface glycoprotein and functions as a cell-cell adhesion factor. It may also mediate the attachment of stem cells to bone marrow extracellular matrix or directly to stromal cells. The concern about cells expressing CD34+ marker would mean contamination of the MSC culture with other cells like fibroblast which express the molecule CD34+.

Placenta and Amniotic fluid

Recent studies show that amniotic fluid contains a considerable quantity of stem cells. These amniotic stem cells are pluripotent and able to differentiate into various tissues, which may be useful for future human application. Some researchers, including *Anthony Atala* of Wake Forest University, a team from Harvard University, and Italian Paolo de Coppi, have found that amniotic fluid is also a plentiful source of non-embryonic stem cells. These cells have demonstrated the ability to differentiate into a number of different cell-types, including brain, liver and bone. The placenta is a much better source of stem cells since it contains up to ten times more than cord blood. Some placental blood may be returned to the neonatal circulation if the umbilical cord is not prematurely clamped.

Adipose Tissue

Adult stem cells (ASCs), originally identified as a source of osteoprogenitor cells, MSCs differentiate into adipocytes, chondrocytes, osteoblasts and myoblasts in vitro and undergo differentiation in vivo making these stem cells promising candidates for mesodermal defect repair and disease management. However, the clinical use of MSCs has presented problems, including pain, morbidity and low cell number upon havest. This has led to researchers to investigate alternate sources for MSCs.

Adipose tissue, like bone marrow, is derived from the mesenchyme and contains a supportive stroma that is easily isolated. Based on this, adipose tissue may represent a source of stem cells that could have far-reaching effects on several fields. Compared to any other source, the high concentrations of generative cells found in adipose tissue, especially in the abdominal region, by sheer volume of availability, ensure an abundance in the number of ASCs ranging in the millions per unit volume. The sheer number available also has the added advantage of not needing to be cultured in a laboratory over days in order to get the desired number of ASCs to achieve therapeutic threshold.

Adipose tissue ASCs (AT-ASCs) are extremely similar to stem cells isolated from bone marrow (BMASCs). The similarities in profile between the types of ASCs range from morphology to growth to transcriptional and cell surface phenotypes. Their similarity extends also to their developmental behavior both in vitro and in vivo. This has led to suggestions that adipose-derived stem cells are in fact a mesenchymal stem cell fraction present within adipose tissue. Clinically, however, stromal vascular fraction-derived AT-ASCs have the advantage over their bone marrow-derived counterparts, because of their abundance in numbers, eliminating the need for culturing over days to obtain a therapeutically viable number and the ease of the harvest procedure being less painful than harvest of bone marrow.

This in theory means that an autologous transplant of adipose-derived ASCs will not only work in much the same way as the successes shown using marrow-derived mesenchymal stem cell transplant, but also be of minimal risk to the patient. AT-ASCs, like BM-ASCs, are called mesenchymal ASCs because they are both of mesodermal germ origin. This means that AT-ASCs are able to differentiate into specialized cells of mesodermal origin such as adipocytes, fibrocytes, fibroblasts, myocytes, osteocytes and chondrocytes.

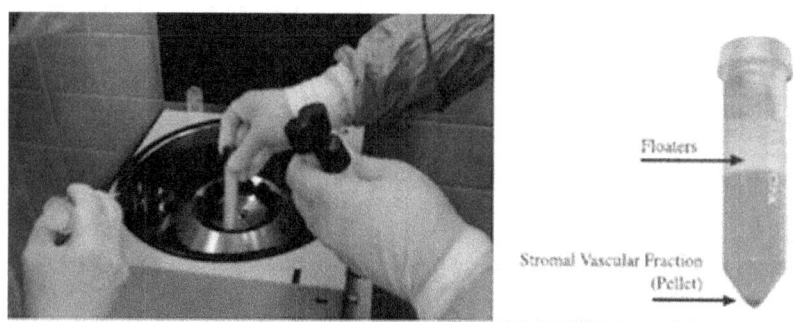

Figure 3. Separation of Adult Stem Cells from Adipose Tissue.

Chapter 4

Clinical Trials

Clinical trials are sets in medical research and drug development that generate safety and efficacy data or more specifically, information about adverse drug reactions and adverse effects of other treatments for health interventions. They are conducted only after satisfactory information has been gathered on the quality of the non clinical safety and health authority/ethics committee approval is granted in the country where approval of the drug or device is sought.

Investigators initially enroll volunteers and /or patients into small studies and subsequently conduct larger scale studies in patients that often compare the new product with others already approved for the affliction of interest. Clinical trials often involve patients with specific health conditions who then benefit from receiving otherwise unavailable treatments.

A discussion from the Drake Institute in regards to 'clinical trials' states that clinical trials have no place in stem cell studies because each patient can serve as his/her own control. With all the modern technology for objective assessment of a patient's medical condition, there is no need for a randomized study. Each patient can be carefully evaluated before and after treatment, by objective medical testing using various equipment, and their condition after therapy compared to that before. Clinical trial format is not relevant nor applicable to patient specific therapy involving adult stem cells or even adult fetal stem cells.

This type of experimentation is certainly appropriate for animals but not humans, stem cell therapy does not involve any drug. Particularly with respect to the injection of autologous stem cells, that are found naturally in the patient, the patient is receiving what one already has, just more of it, in a clinical trial half the patients are chosen at random to receive a placebo, while half of the patients are given an experimental drug, clinical trials are not necessary for stem cell treatments because stem cells are not drugs.

Many studies that have been conducted are proof enough that clinical trials for stem cells are not required, in particular, a study carried out by Suphachai *Chaithiraphan et al* 2009 in Thailand where blood-borne angiogenic cell precursors (ACPs) harvested from patient's peripheral bood, cultured and expanded and later injected intracoronarly in patients who were considered in advanced-stage ischemic heart disease.

Informed consent was obtained from all patients before the procedure. This clinical study was a non-randomized open study of consecutive patients with chronic coronary artery disease. Clinical trials are not necessary for stem cell treatments because the cells used in most cases are autologous stem cells. Autologous transplant is a type of transplant that uses the patient's own stem cells. These cells are collected in advance and returned to the patient at a later stage. They are used to replace stem cells that have been damaged by high doses of chemotherapy or to treat the patient's underlying disease.

Autologous transplants are used to treat a number of different blood cancers, leukaemias lymphomas, myeloma, certain solid tumors, breast cancer, testicular cancer osteosarcoma and a lot more diseases.

Stem cells used in autologous transplant are adult stem cells, these are cells that can make identical copies of themselves for long periods of time, this ability to proliferate is referred to as long-term self-renewal. Adult stem cells can give rise to mature cell types that have characteristic morphologies and specialized functions.

Their primary function is to maintain a steady state functioning of a cell called homeostasis and with limitations, to replace cells that die because of injury or disease. Adult stem cells are dispersed in tissues throughout the mature animal and behave very differently depending on their local environment.

Chapter 5

Patient specific Trials

There are stem cells in every body's body that can be used to treat or manage an individual's medical condition. In many situations they only have to be harvested, isolated, slightly improved or grown to larger numbers and then placed back in the right spot in the right way. Since these are not mass-produced drugs, but your own body tissues, applying a mass-manufacture regulatory regime to your cells makes no common sense, yet that's what the FDA, big pharma and major universities want. Since your Doctor using your stem cells as body tissues instead of drugs spells financial ruin to them.

Stem cells are cells that are capable of turning into other types of cells to help repair damaged tissue, they are all over our bodies, in almost every tissue. The commonly used stem cells in therapy are adult stem cells (ASCs) which have no negative stigma that pervaded embryonic stem cell research. Stem cell therapy is typically autologous, meaning the cells are taken from one's own body and then re-injected back into a specific area to be treated. No embryos are harmed, and the cells come directly from the person being treated. Autologous ASCs have emerged as a viable form of treatment for a number of diseases and conditions.

Since in traditional clinical trials, not all the participants receive the drug under study, the FDA does give approval to institutions involved in the approval of scientific study protocols involving human subjects, these could include Science and Ethics Committees, Hospitals, manufacturing companies and Institutional Review Boards (IRB). This has made it possible patient specific clinical trials, also called ''patient sponsored'' studies.

Such studies with autologous stem cells do not require government sponsorship, the patient pays for the study, there is no randomized or double blind study, every patient receives the treatment and both doctor and the patient know they are receiving the treatment and what the treatment is.

There are several patient sponsored autologous stem cell treatment studies in the USA that meets the current FDA guidance and requirements. One study conductd by a US based company called Bioheart has conducted a patient specific stem cell treatment for Diabetes type II, in conjunction with Repair Stem Cell Institute starting in April 2014.

The Food and Drug Administration's (FDA) view on Clinical use of Stem Cell

Stem cell treatment centers in the USA have been faced with challenges in regards to access to stem cell therapy for every one due to FDA regulatory laws which have been made to regard autologous stem cells as drugs. This translates to saying that if your cells are drugs, you no longer control them and their use, instead, their use would be governed by federal drug laws rather than your needs. Under current regulatory, policy, even if the cells in your body could be used by your Doctor to save your life one day, you legally do not have the right to use them for that purpose if FDA requirements are not met.

The FDA has always claimed that there isn't enough research and clinical trials to substantiate the use of stem cells in therapy. The truth of the matter is that there is currently over 167, 879 published studies on stem cells listed in the USA national library of medicine. Just on mesenchymal stem cells alone there is17,632 studies available. For comparison purposes, there are only 13,118 papers investigating the use of the most commonly used antibiotic, amoxicillin, for which 52.3 million prescriptions were written in 2010. The newly approved immunology drug, belimumab, there are only 140 research papers listed, in terms of the volume of published knowledge, there is approximately 12,500 more known about a single adult stem cell type than this newly approved drug.

By 2009, there had already been more than15,000 cord blood transplants worldwide. In the USA, more than one-half of all stem cell transplants from unrelated donors in children now use cord blood. Most pediatric patients who have received cord blood transplants were affected by leukemia, lymphoma, servere aplastic anaemia, and other lethal diseases of the blood or immune system as well as certain inherited metabolic diseases. Despite the fact that cord blood banks have been saving lives with this tissue, for more than a decade, the FDA announced in 2009 that cord blood should be treated as a drug. As a result, the costs to obtain cord blood have markedly increased while the safety profile remains unchanged.

Adipose cells are processed at the bed side during fat-transfer surgeries where a surgeon moves fat from one part of the body and places it in another. The basic

23

procedure has been performed for more than a century. However, the FDA has asserted that if the structure of the fat is broken down, as is common in a new same day stem cell procedure being performed by physicians, then this creates a drug of the patient's own cells. The FDA's Tissue Reference Group (TRG) has sent letters to physicians performing adipose cell transfers, stating that even if they process these cells during the same surgical procedure in their offices with no culture involved, the practice is still creating a new drug.

The FDA has much less stringent regulations if, for example, a company wants to sell cadaver bone for use in surgery in that these products aren't treated the same as a new drug, the only requirement is that you follow a minimal set of safety standards processing the tissue and you test for communicable diseases.

A company called Cytori Therapeautics, created a new device to process fat to isolate stem cells resident in the tissue, this is a simple process, and in Europe, the machine was quickly granted approval. In the USA, however, the part of the FDA that regulates stem cells has made it a nightmare to get the machine approved. While the FDA admitted the machine does what it says it should do and produces a mix of cells free from contamination, it claimed that since the product of the machine was the patient's own stem cell mix, it would consider the machine the same as a new drug. The big concern raised was that the machine's stem cell mix could be used off-label by a Doctor.

Chapter 6

Current USA Stem Cells Treatment

The United States Food and Drug Administration (FDA) claims that a patient's own stem cells are a drug which it intends to regulate. This means that clinical trials are required and a physician must submit his treatment for approval. Since it was enacted in 1938, the Food, Drug, and Cosmetic Act (FDCA) has regulated medical drugs and devices based on basic public health concepts that recognize the differences between the practice of medicine and mass production of drugs. The regulation of mass manufactured and widely distributed medical products led to a revolution in healthcare that greatly increased public safety and unquestionably saved lives due to the reduction of unsafe products.

Things changed in 2006, when the FDA, without public commentary, altered a single word in its regulatory language regarding cell and tissue based therapies that moved their focus from protecting the public from communicable disease transmission to asserting authority over virtually all therapies using autologous cells and tissue. Most organizations have noted that the FDA was only granted authority by the U.S Congress to regulate allogeneic tissue transplants in order to control communicable disease transmission and that the Agency had no authority to regulate human cells of any type like mass produced prescription drugs. Other organizations have indicated that stem cell transplants are medical procedures, their use is the practice of medicine, not the manufacturing of a drug as the FDA asserts.

In 2008, the FDA sent a notice to Regenerative Sciences, a medical practice that utilized expanded bone marrow derived mesenchymal stem cells for autologous orthopedic use. The FDA asserted that their drug mass production rules applied to the practices at the clinic. The Agency has recently made a worrisome assertion about the processing of adipose tissue, a medical practice that has been around for more than 100 years. The claim is that, any isolation of the stem cell rich fraction of fatty tissue for orthopedic use by physician for his or her own use in patients equates to the manufacture of a drug, even if that tissue is processed at the bedside. Congress had only authorized the FDA classify a substance that affected the body through ''chemical action'' as a drug, the Agency needed to clarify its position as to why a patient's own stem cells could be considered a drug. The Agency responded by saying that ''when living cells interact with their environment to mediate repair and/or generate damaged tissue, they do so by chemical action.'' The Regenexx procedures are a family of non-surgical stem cell and blood platelet treatments for common injuries and degenerative joint conditions, such as osteoarthritis and avascular necrosis. These stem cell procedures utilize a patient's own stem cells or blood platelets to help heal damaged tissues, tendons, ligaments, cartilage, spinal disc or bone. It works by taking a blood sample and a bone marrow sample from a patient and separating out stem cells via centrifuge, then re-infuse those cells directly into the injured area where they assimulate into the bone or cartilage and begin to regenerate it.

Regulators have argued that the Regenexx procedure is equivalent to the administration of a drug because the stem cells that are re-injected into patients constitute an article that is intended to treat, cure and mitigate diseases and to affect the structure and function of the patient's body, therefore fitting within the definition of 'drug'.

Chapter 7

International Stem centers by country

Special thanks goes to all the treatment centers that were kind enough to share information about their treatment centers, this information is meant to assist both physicians and patients who seek stem cell treatment to quickly identify treatment centers that may be suitable for their needs because not all stem cell treatment centers can treat all conditions.

Most of the stem cell treatment centers listed in this chapter are those that were contacted through email and other means, it is worth mentioning that some centers are also included because most of the required information to guide a patient or physician is available in the center's web page and some centers, especially those that have treatment centers in multiple countries, failed to share the information required for this reference because they felt that instead of reaching the centers through the contact or spoke's person for the treatment centers, they tend to visit the stem cell treatment centers direct, this may not be good business for those using the centers as income generation source. Since this is a first edition of such a compilation of International Stem Cell Treatment centers, it is hoped that more information on centers that failed to respond before this publication will be included in the second edition of this reference. It is worth mentioning that this reference does not include accreditation/good standing of these centers with regulatory bodies within their countries.

1. United States of America (USA)

Name

Stem Cell Rejuvenation Center

Website

http://www.center.com/FAQ.html

Physical Address

7600 N. 15th Street Ste. 102

Phoenix, AZ 85020

Telephone

(602)439-0000 office

(602)439-0021 fax

Contact Person

Josh

Email

info@the-stem-cell-center.com

Diseases/conditions Treated

1. ALS
2. Alzheimer's
3. Autism
4. Cerebral Palsy
5. Degenerative Disc Disease
6. Erectile dysfunction
7. Glaucoma
8. Hearing loss
9. Heart disease
10. Huntington Disease

11.Kidney failure
12.Liver Disease
13.Macular Degeneration
14.Muscular Dystrophy
15.Optic nerve injury
16.Parkinson's Disease
17.Pulmonary Fibrosis
18.Renitinitis Pigmentosa
19.Spinal cord injury
20.Stroke
21.Diabeties
22.Lupus
23.Multiple scleroses
24.Rhematoid arthritis

Source/Type of stem cells used

Autologous Adipose Stem Cells

Procedure/Protocol used

A small sample of adipose tissue is removed from above the superior iliac spine or abdomen under local anesthetic. Adipose tissue contains much larger volumes of mesenchymal stem cells than does bone marrow extraction.

Estimated Costs

Stem Cell consultation and treatment: $7,600.00

Name

(b). Regenexx Stem Cell Treatment Center/Centeno-Schultz Clinic

Website

www.regenexx.com

Physical Address

403 Summit Blvd., Suite 201

Broomfield, CO 80021

Telephone

303-495-4014

Toll Free: 1-888-525-3005

Contact Person/Patient Liaison

Che DeMarco

Diseases Treated

1. Degenerative joint conditions
2. Common injuries
3. Osteoarthritis
4. Vascular necrosis
5. Arthritis

Source of Stem Cells

Autologous Blood sample and bone marrow

Treatment Costs

Range from $4000 - $8000

Procedure/Protocol

Regenexx works by taking a blood sample and a bone marrow sample from a patient and separating out the stem cells via centrifugation, then re-injecting those cells directly into the injured area, where they assimilate into the bone or cartilage and begin to regenerate it.

Name

(c). Miami Stem Cell Treatment Center

Website

http://www.miamistemcellsusa.com

Physical Address

Boca Raton

Miami Stem Cell Treatment Center

1515 North Federal Highway

Suite 105

Boca Raton, Florida, 33432

Telephone

(561) 331-2999

Fax

(561) 331-2998

(Miami Stem Cell Treatment Center comprises of 4 others centers, reachable at the same phone numbers)

Contact Person (s)

Nicole Rintrona

Dr. Thomas A. Gionis

Dr. Nia Smyrniotis

Email

Dr.Gionis@MiamistemCellsUsa.com

Dr.Nia@MiamiStemCellsUsa.com

Diseases/Medical conditions Treated

1. Cardiac –Pulmonary
2. Neurologic
3. Orthopedic
4. Spine
5. Autoimmune Diseases

Sources of Stem Cells

Adult Autologous Aipose-derived Stem Cells (ADSCs)

Cost

$8,900

Procedure/Protocol

The stem cells come from stromal vascular fraction (SVF), a protein rich segment from processed adipose tissue. Stromal vascular fraction contains a mononuclear cell line predominantly with mesenchymal stem cells, macrophages, endothelial cells, and growth factors that facilitate the stem cell processes and promote their activity. The SVF is harvested, concentrated, then deployed back into the patient's body via injection or intravenous infusion on an outpatient bases.

Name

(d). Northwest University, Feinberg School of Medicine

Division of Immunotherapy and Autoimmune Diseases (DIAD)

Website

Http://www.stemcell-immunotherapy.com

Physical Address

Division of Immunotherapy and Autoimmune Diseases

Northwest University, Feinberg School of Medicine

446 E Ontario ste 10-1000

Chicago, IL 60611

Contact Person

Ms. Kate Quigley

Telephone

312-695-4960

312-695-4961 (fax)

Email

info@stemcell-immunotherapy.com

Diseases/Conditions Treated

1. Autoimmune Bullous skin disorders
2. Retinopathy and Optic Neuropathy
3. Chronic Inflammatory Demyelinating Polynaropathy
4. Crohn's Devic's Disease
5. Idiopathic Inflammatory Myopathy Disease

6. Leukocyte Adhesion Deficiency Type 1
7. Multiple Sclerosis
8. Myasthenia Gravis
9. Primary Biliary Cirrhosis
10. Pulmonary Fibrosis
11. Rheumatoid Arthritis
12. Sarcaidosis
13. Scleroderma
14. Systemic Lupus Erythematosus
15. Systemic Necrotizing Vasculitis
16. Morphea
17. Type 1 Diabetes

Sources of Stem Cells used

1. Peripheral Blood
2. Umbilical Cord Blood

Treatment Cost

Not provided

Procedure/Protocol

Treatment protocol includes four phases:

Phase I: Pre-transplant Testing include MRI, CT, scans, Blood work, Pulmonary function tests. This is followed by admission to the hospital overnight for chemotherapy, then discharged the following day after fluid hydration.

Phase II: After being discharged, the patient gives himself/herself the shorts to grow stem cells (neupogen)

Phase III: Stem cells are collected by apheresis.

Phase IV: The patient is admitted to the hospital for transplant. The patient receives IV fluids followed by chemotherapy and receiving his/her stem cells (similar to blood transfusion)

2. Argentina

Name of treatment center

Fernandez Vina Foundation

Physical Address

The legal Address for this center is that of the Contact Person;

Don Margolis

Repair Stem Cell Institute

3010 LBj Freeway, Suit 1200

Dallas, TX75234

Telephone

(214) 556-6377

Email

donmargolis@gmail.com

Diseases/Conditions Treated

1. Heart Disease
2. Lung Disease
3. Diabetes

Source of stem cells

Bone marrow autologous stem cells

Treatment Costs

$14,900

3. Panama

Treatment Center

Panama Stem Cell Institute

Website

Http://www.cellmedicine.com

Physical Address

Plaza Pacific Office #2A

Via Israel Calle 66y 67

Via Israel, Ciadad de Panama

Panama

Contact person

Dr. Neil H. Riordan

Diseases/Conditions

1. Autism
2. Cerebral Palsy
3. Heart Failure
4. Multiple Sclerosis
5. Osteoarthritis
6. Rheumatoid Arthritis
7. Spinal Cord Injury
8. Autoimmune Diseases

Source of Stem Cells

1. Bone marrow
2. Adipose Tissue
3. Cord Blood

Treatment Cost

Not provided

Procedure/Protocol

Type of stem cells used and protocol used may depend upon individual condition. What is interesting will the protocols for the conditions treated by this center is that Umbilical Cord Blood is used in all the protocols.

For Autism, CP, and Heart disease, the source of stem cells used is allogeneic Umbilical Cord Blood. This cord blood come from donated umbilical cords. Because HLA matching is not necessary, anyone can be treated with allogeneic cord blood. Allogeneic stem cells can be administered multiple times over the course of days in uniform dosages that contain high level counts. Umbilical cord tissue provides an abundant supply of mesenchymal stem cell. Protocols include three phases, 4 infusion of allogeneic mesenchymal stem cells, 2 infusion of allogeneic mesenchymal stem cells and two, 2 infusion of mesenchymal stem cells followed by 1 infusion at two intervals. For MS, Osteoarthritis, Rheumatoid Arthritis and Autoimmune disease, the stem cells used are Fat tissue and Umbilical Cord and the procedure of administering is the same. For treating spinal cord injury, the stem cell source is the bone marrow and cord blood.

4. India

Treatment Center

Chaitanya Stem Cell Center

Website

Http://www.chaitanyastemcell.com

Physical Address

Rahi Sakha Apt S.No. 133

Pune-Sinhagad Road, Parrati

Pune 411030

Contact Person

Anant Bagul

Email

anantbagul@yahoo.com

Telephone

020-243329666

+91 9011-111-222 (mobile)

Diseases/conditions Treated

1. Autoimmune
2. Eye conditions
3. Paediatric neurological disorders
4. Metabolic diseases

5. Chronic Kidney disease
6. Antiaging
7. Chacort Mariet tooth
8. Liver
9. Polio

Source of Stem Cell

Fetal Stem Cell

Treatment Cost

Not provided

5. Israel

Name of Treatment Center

International Center for Cell Therapy and Cancer Immunology

Website

http://www.ctcicenter.com

Physical Address

Weizmann Center

20th floor – Top Ichilov

14 Weizmann Street

Tel Aviv 64239

Israel

Contact Person

Ruth Grunbaum

Email

info@ctcicenter.com

Telephone

Phone +972 77 777 9255

Fax +972 77 777 9247

Diseases/Conditions Treated

1. Hodgin's Disease
2. Myelodysplastic syndromes
3. Multiple Myeloma
4. Hematological solid tumors
5. Chemoresistant metastatic solid tumors

6. Multiple Sclerosis
7. Aplastic Anamia
8. Fanconi's anemia
9. SCID
10. Spinal cord injury
11. Parkinson's
12. Stroke
13. Autism
14. SLE
15. Crohn's disease
16. Beta Thalassemia
17. Sickle cell anemia
18. Gaucher's disease
19. Hurler's disease
20. Metachromatic leukodystrophy etc.

Source of Stem cells used

1. Autologous mesenchymal stem cells isolated from bone marrow or adipose tissue

Treatment Cost

Not provided

Procedure/Protocol

Transplants may be autologous or from cells cryopreserved cord blood or allogeneic cells

The bone marrow transplant procedure is used to restore a patient's immune system after intence chemotherapy directed at a serious cancer like leukemia has destroyed the patient's immune system. It is directed at re-establishing an effective immune system by using a donor's healthy immune cells to augment the patient's own immune system without the donor cells being rejected, to strengthen the patient's own cancer defense response.

A fully myeloablative bone marrow transplantation procedure is performed in a hospital under clean and isolated conditions since the patient 's own immune system is destroyed by the process, and the patient has no natural defenses during the period it takes for the transplanted stem cells to create new functioning white blood cells. CTCI also provides several types of dendritic cell therapeutic vaccines which patients take after they already have cancer. These therapeutic vaccines are made from two main ingredients, dendritic cells plus antigens (biomarkers) of the cancer being treated. The biomarkers are obtained from the patient's own tumor tissue, if not, they are obtained from a bank or library. Dendritic vaccines are designed to activate dendritic cells, so that they can accomplish the mobilization of the whole immune system.

6. Thailand

Name of Treatment center

Stem Cells Thailand

Website

http://stemcellthailand.org

Contact Person

Not provided

Diseases/Conditions treated

1. Heart diseases
2. Kidney disease
3. Autism Spectrum
4. Brain injuries
5. Cerebral Palsy
6. Fibromyanlgia
7. Cartilage and ligament
8. Alzheimers
9. Rett syndrome
10. Spinocerebral ataxia
    And many more

Sources of Stem Cells

1. Adipose tissue
2. Umbilical cord
3. Bone marrow

Treatment Cost

$16,000

Procedure/Protocol

Administering the autologous stem cells back to the patient takes a minimum of seven steps:

1. Liposuction to collect at least 100 to 300cc of fat from the patients abdomen or high thigh
2. Breaking down and separation of the adipose tissue using a patented collagenase based solution
3. Using a flow cytometer, the stromal vascular fraction (SVF) is separated
4. Adult stem cells and progenitor cells are isolated from the SVF
5. The adult stem cells are then cleaned/washed to remove any left over collagenase
6. The isolated cells are suspended with the patient's Platelet Rich Plasma (PRP) with other growth factors to activate the dormant cells
7. Lastly, the stem cells are then injected back to the patient through intravenous drips.

7.China

Hope Medical Group/Stem Cells for Hope

Stem cells for Hope Inc. has an international network of clinics around the world including China. This treatment center is offering stem cell treatment using autologous adult stem cells or from harvested Cord Blood Stem Cells. The Hope Treatment Center is a US based company, however, Stem Cell for Hope does not have any treatment facilities nor do they treat any patient inside the United States, however, applications for treatment can still be handled in the US, and then referred to a relevant treatment center outside the USA.

Website

http://www.hopestemcell.com

Physical Address

4474 Middle Country Road

Calverton, NY 11933

USA

Tel: (631) 929- 3900

Fax: (631) 929- 3909

Email

info@hopestemcell.com

Diseases/Conditions Treated

1. Multiple Sclerosis
2. Parkinson's Disease
3. Stroke
4. Macular Degeneration
5. Optic nerve damage
6. Optic Neuritis

7. Liver cirrhosis
8. Crohn's Disease
9. Hematopoietic stem cell transplantation
10. Cardiovascular and cerebrovascular diseases intervention therapy
11. Other conditions are evaluated for treatment on a per case bases

Sources of Stem Cells Used

1. Cord Blood

Treatment Cost

Not provided

Procedure/Protocol

Umbilical Cord Stem Cells or Dendritic cells plus Cancer Killer Cells, and neurological approaches to treat a wide range of neurological disorders as well as cancer and other diseases. Scientists from National Institute of Health (NIH), instead of using surgery, chemotherapy or radiotherapy, are using CIK immunotherapy to attack tumors. CIK has proved in medical practice to be the most efficiently adopted immunotherapy. It shows good efficacies in treating malignant tumors in leukemia, melanoma, malignant lymphoma, renal cell carcinoma, metastatic renal carcinoma, lung cancer and gastric cancer.

8. Repair Stem Cell Institute (RSCI)

RSCI is one of the largest Adult Stem Cell treatment institute with many treatment centers around the world, in countries like Argentina, Mexico, Thailand, Philipines, United States of America and many more. RSCI is using adult stem cell treatment to treat over 150 debilitating chronic conditions previously thought to be untreatable such as the 'Big Three' – Heart Disease, Diabetes and Lung Disease, as well as Ataxia, Parkinson's Disease, Spinal Cord Injury, Cerebral Palsy, Multiple Sclerosis, Arthritis and Autism. More on RSCI centers in chapter 8.

Website

http://repairstemcells.org

Physical Address

Repair Stem Cells Institute

3010 LBJ Freeway, Suite 1200

Dallas, TX 75234

Telephone

(214) 556-6377

Contact Person

Don Margolis

Email

donmargolis@gmail.com

Sources of Stem Cells used

1. Umbilical Cord Blood
2. Bone Marrow
3. Adipose Tissue

Treatment Cost

Dependent upon the treatment center and the condition (s) being treated, otherwise, costs may be around $14,500 (see some treatment costs by treatment center in chapter 8).

Chapter 8

Stem Cell Treatment Centers recommended by Repair Stem Cell Institute (RSCI)

The RSCI has worked tirelessly to find the top stem cell treatment centers worldwide. All centers recommended by RSCI and physicians meet the highest standards to ensure the safest and most effective therapy for their patients.

All international stem cell treatment centers, physicians and supplying laboratories approved by RSCI must meet the following conditions;

Treatment Centers:

1. Must be licensed, certified and in good-standing with the country's medical professional regulatory board.
2. Must have at least one year's experience treating human patients with Repair Stem Cells, also known as Adult Stem Cells
3. Must never have received a negative finding from a regulatory inquiry or governmental action concerning patient relations or marketplace fraud.
4. Must use either the patient's own stem cells or Cord Blood stem cells derived from the umbilical cords of newborn babies, including Umbilical Cord Blood stem cells derived from placentas of healthy newborns. In certain cases, cells from other donors, whether stem cells or plain cells may be used. RSCI will not recommend any center using fetal or embryonic stem cells to treat any disease.

Physicians:

1. Received honoraria or doctorates from at least two recognized academic institutions
2. Participated in a successful Adult Stem Cell clinical trial
3. Authored a published, peer-reviewed article on Repair Stem Cells
4. Received a grant for Adult Stem Cell research from a government unit and /or a recognized charity/disease advocacy organization
5. Presented a paper on stem cell treatment at a professional conference

Laboratories producing ASC for RCSI stem cell treatment centers:

1. Have a history of over 100 successful repair stem cell human implants
2. Meet the minimum recognized Current Good Manufacturing Procedure (CGMP) standards.

Stem Cell Treatment Centers recommended by RSCI include the following:

1. Clinica San Nicholas in Buenos Aires, Argentina. The founder is Dr. Roberto Fernandez Vina. Dr. Vina is well known as the world's number one stem cell cardiologist and diabetes stem cell specialist.

Amongst a variety of diseases treated at the center, a six day stem cell treatment program for Diabetes, Lung and Heart Diseases is being offered at $14,900 including accommodation for the patient and companion.

Some, just to mention a few of Dr. Vina's numerous achievements include the first implant of stem cells during pump cardiac surgery, first trial of injection of stem cells directly into the heart, first implant of autologous stem cells in the pancreas to treat Diabetes 1 &2, first stem cell treatments for Chronic Obstructive Pulmonary Disease (COPD).

2. Bioheart Company, a USA based company, this center has in April 2014 assembled doctors and specialists trained in stem cell treatments for a treatment study using autologous adult stem cells which was available to the general public. The study was a patient-sponsored research study for treatment of type 2 Diabetes. The treatment was available for only $5000.

3. The Philipines, Manila, Dr. Florencio Q. Lucero pioneered the use of Adipose or fat Adult Stem Cell Treatment for Diabetes in 2006. Dr. Lucero is a seasoned plastic surgeon with 34 years of private practice in Manila and in Dubai. To date, he has conducted clinical studies on 30 Diabetes patients and more than 300 patients with various degenerative conditions, all of whom showed remarkable improvements in their medical conditions. Stem Cell Clinical Trials conducted includes the following;

- The Efficacy safety of Autologous Fat Stem Cell Transplant in the management of type 1 and type 2 Diabetes Mellitus
- The Efficacy and safety of sheep placental Stem Cell activator in facial rejuvenation
- Cosmetic application of platelet rich plasma as stem cell activator in facial rejuvenation

4. Lauderdale, Florida, USA, the RSCI announced its new stem cell program for the treatment of Spinal Cord Injuries (SCI). The regenerative center is headed by Dr. Melvin M. Propis, a well known practitioner of stem cells science

References

1. Akimoto Nimura, Koji Otabe, Hedeyuki Koga, Young-Jin Jun: Analysis of Human synovial and bone marrow mesenchymal stem cells in relation to heat-inactivation of autologous and fetal bovine serums. *BMC MusculoskeletalDisorders* 2010, 11:208

2. Andrew JG, Hoyland JA, Freemont AJ et al.: Platelet derived growth factor expression in normally healing human fractures. *Bone*. 1995 16: 455-460.

3. Canango PM, Lekovie V, Weinlaender M, et al.: Platelet- rich plasma and bovine porous bone mineral combined with guided tissue regeneration in the treatment of intrabony defects in humans. *J Periodontal Res*. 2002 37:300-3006.

4. Christopher J. Centeno: The Stem Cells they don't want you to have. 2012

5. Elizabeth Csaszar, Daniel C. Kirouac, Mei Yu, Weijia Wang, Wenlian Qiao: Rapid Expansion of Human Hematopoietic Stem Cells by Automated Control of Inhibitory Feedback Signaling

6. Friedenstein AJ, Petrakova KV, Kurolesova AI, et al.: Analysis of precursor cells for osteogenic and hematopoietic tissues. Transplantation 6:230-247. Garg AK,: The use of Platelet-rich plasma to enhance the success of bone grafts around dental implants. *Dent Implantol Update*. 2000, 11:17-21.

7. Garg AK,: The use of Platelet-rich plasma to enhance the success of bone grafts around dental implants. *Dent Implantol Update*. 2000, 11:17-21. Hakimi M, Jungbluth P, Sager M, et al.: Combined use of platelet-rich plasma and autologus bone grafts in the treatment of long bone defects in mini-pigs. *Injury*. 2010, 41:717-723.

8. Ichiro Sekiya, Benjamin L. Larson, Jason R. Smith, Radhika Pochampally, Jian-Guo Cui, Darwin J. Prockop: Expansion of Human Adult Stem Cells from bone marrow stroma: conditions that maximize the yields of early progenitors and evaluate their quality.2002. *DOI:10.1634/stemcells*.20-6-530

9. Jennifer Antonchuk, Guy Sauvageau, Keith Humphries: HOXB4-Induced Expansion of Adult Hematopoietic Stem Cells ex vivo. Cell, Vol. 109, 39-45 April 5, 2002 Joyce ME, Jingushi S, Bolander ME,: Transforming growth factor-beta in the regulation of fracture repair. *Orthop Clin North AM*. 1990, 21: 199-209.

10. Marcola et al: Case Dismissed! Texas ends 15 year fight against cancer doctor Burzynski.January19, 2013. *Marcola.com*: 364, 332

11. Melanie Vogl, Johannes Fischer, Marcus Jager, Christoph Zilkens, Rudiger Krauspe, Monika Herten: Can thrombin-activated platelet releasate compensate the age-induced decrease in cell proliferation of MSC? June 2013.DOI 10.1002/jor.22433.

12. Michael Freeman, Mitchell Fuerst: Does the FDA have regulatory authority over adult autologous stem cell therapies? 21 CFR 1271 and the emperor's new clothes. *Freeman and Fruerst Journal of Transplantational Medicine* 2012, 10:60

13. Neil Riordan, Kyle Chan, Annette M. Marleau, Thomas E. Ichim; Cord blood in regenerative medicine: do we need immune suppression? Journal of Transfusion Medicine 2007, 5:8 doi: 10.1186/1479-5876-5-8

14. Patricia A. Zuk, Min Zhu, Peter Ashjian, Daniel A. DeUgarte, Jerry I. Huang, Hiroshi Mizuno, Zeni C. Alfonso, John K. Fraser, Prosper Benhaim, and Marc H. Hedrick: Human Adipose Tissue is a source of Multipotent Stem Cells. *Mol Bio Cell*. 2002 Dec. 13(12): 4279-4295.

15. Vanderson Rocha, Myriam Labopin, Guillermo Sanz, William Arcese, Rainer Schwerdtfeger, Alberto Bosi, Niels Jacobsen, Tapani Ruutu, Marcos de Lima, Jurgen Finke, Francesco Frassoni, Eliane Gluckman: Transplants of Umbilical-Cord Blood or bone marrow from unrelated donors in adults with acute leukemia. *N Engl j.Med 2004; 351:2276-85*